MERIWETHER LEWIS AND WILLIAM CLARK

Rachel Lynette

PowerKiDS press

New York

For Emily

Published in 2014 by The Rosen Publishing Group, Inc.
29 East 21st Street, New York, NY 10010

First Edition

Editor: Jennifer Way
Book Design: Greg Tucker
Layout Design: Andrew Povolny

Photo Credits: Cover, p. 5 David David Gallery/Superstock/Getty Images; p. 6 Mansell/Time & Life Pictures/Getty Images; pp. 7, 10 North Wind Picture Archives/AP Images; p. 9 Photos.com/Thinkstock; p. 11 Superstock/Getty Images; p. 12 AP Photo/Stephanie S. Cordle; p. 13 DEA/G. Dagli Orti/De Agostini Picture Library/Getty Images; p. 15 Richard Cummins/Lonely Planet Images/Getty Images; p. 16 Dan Thornberg/Shutterstock.com; p. 18 Shane W. Thompson/Shutterstock.com; p. 19 AP Photo/The Billings Gazette/Bob Zellar; pp. 21, 22 Jean-Erick Pasquier/Gamma-Rapho/Getty Images.

Library of Congress Cataloging-in-Publication Data

Lynette, Rachel.
 Meriwether Lewis and William Clark / by Rachel Lynette. — First edition.
    pages cm. — (Pioneer spirit: the westward expansion)
 Includes index.
 ISBN 978-1-4777-0783-8 (library binding) — ISBN 978-1-4777-0899-6 (pbk.) —
ISBN 978-1-4777-0900-9 (6-pack)
 1. Lewis and Clark Expedition (1804–1806)—Juvenile literature. 2. West (U.S.)—Discovery and exploration—Juvenile literature. 3. West (U.S.)—Description and travel—Juvenile literature. 4. Lewis, Meriwether, 1774-1809—Juvenile literature. 5. Clark, William, 1770–1838—Juvenile literature. 6. Explorers—West (U.S.)—Biography—Juvenile literature. I. Title.
 F592.7.L96 2014
 917.804'2—dc23
                        2012048036

Manufactured in the United States of America

CPSIA Compliance Information: Batch #S13PK6: For Further Information contact Rosen Publishing, New York, New York at 1-800-237-9932

CONTENTS

Into the Unknown

In the early 1800s, the land west of the Mississippi River had largely not been explored by Americans, because at the time the United States stretched only to that river. In 1804, Meriwether Lewis and William Clark lead an **expedition** to explore this land. They travelled by boat, horse, and foot all the way to the Pacific Ocean. Along the way, they wrote about the plants, animals, and land they saw. They also met peacefully with many Native American peoples.

The expedition was an important step toward **Westward Expansion**. After Lewis and Clark had reported on what lay beyond the Mississippi, settlers began to move west.

Lewis and Clark traveled from the Mississippi River and the Pacific Ocean. This painting shows them on that journey. Exploring land to report on it is sometimes called surveying.

William Clark

William Clark was born in Virginia on August 1, 1770. He was the ninth of ten children. William's older brothers were sent to school, but the younger children were not. They learned to read, write, and do math from their older brothers.

William Clark

This picture shows William Clark's brother, George Rogers Clark, leading American troops during the American Revolution.

The **American Revolution** began in 1775, when William was five years old. His five older brothers fought in the war. One of his brothers, George Rogers Clark, became a war hero. When William was fourteen years old, the family moved west to settle in Kentucky, at the edge of the western **frontier**. William learned how to **survive** in the wilderness from his brother George.

Meriwether Lewis

Meriwether Lewis was born in Virginia on August 18, 1774. His father died when he was just five years old. Meriwether's mother remarried and moved the family to Georgia. Soon after the move, Meriwether's half brother and half sister were born.

Map of the United States After the American Revolution

On this map you can see how the United States looked around 1790. The Northwest Territory was land given to the United States by Great Britain after the American Revolution.

NH
MA
NY
RI
CT
PA
NJ
DE
MD
VA
NC
SC
GA

Key
U.S. States
Northwest Territory

Meriwether spent a lot of time outdoors as a boy. He often went hunting with his dogs. He became interested in nature. His mother taught him to collect plants that could be used as medicine. When he was thirteen, Meriwether moved back to Virginia to help his uncle manage his family's land and to attend school.

Meriwether Lewis

Meeting in the Military

William Clark **enlisted** in the United States Army in 1789. The Army **stationed** Clark in the Ohio Valley. There, he helped to protect settlers from Native Americans who were angry because they were losing their land to these settlers. Clark was a good soldier, and he was promoted to lieutenant. One of the men he was in charge of was Meriwether Lewis. The two men became good friends.

This painting shows the Battle of Fallen Timbers. This was a 1794 battle between US troops and Native Americans over land in the Northwest Territory. William Clark led men during this battle.

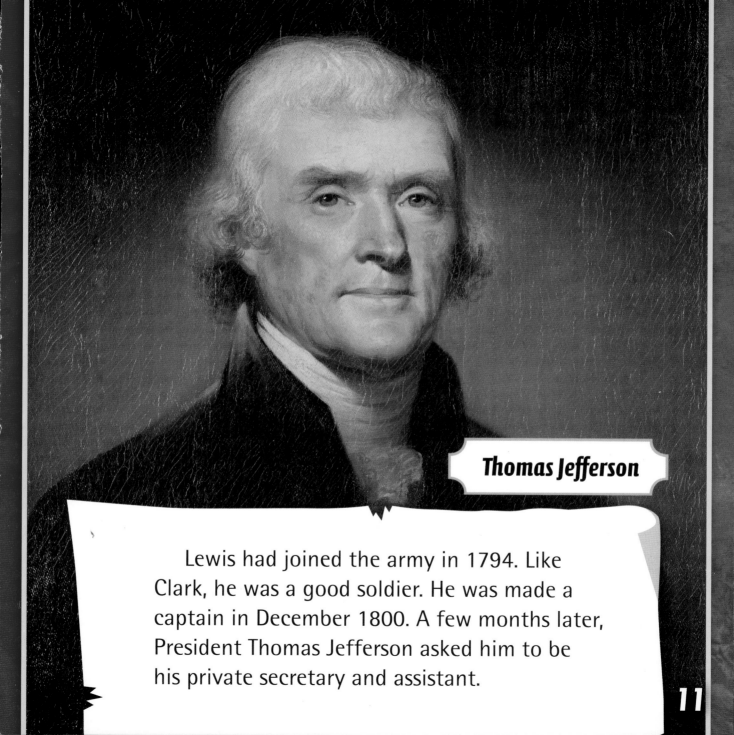

Thomas Jefferson

Lewis had joined the army in 1794. Like Clark, he was a good soldier. He was made a captain in December 1800. A few months later, President Thomas Jefferson asked him to be his private secretary and assistant.

The Corps of Discovery

In 1803, President Jefferson asked Lewis to lead an expedition. The United States had just bought the **Louisiana Territory** from France. Jefferson wanted Lewis to explore this land. Lewis asked Clark to lead the expedition with him.

Lewis and Clark did a lot of work to get ready for the expedition. Lewis studied mapmaking, **botany**, math, and medicine. They bought supplies including tools, food, books, medicines, and presents to give to the Native Americans they would meet.

Lewis and Clark would have used a compass like this one during their expedition.

This painting shows the transfer of ownership of the Louisiana Territory. The French flag is being lowered and the American flag is being raised.

They **recruited** and trained about 38 men, including Clark's slave York, to go with them. Lewis even brought a dog, a Newfoundland named Seaman. The group they formed was called the Corps of Discovery.

The First Year

Lewis and Clark, along with the Corps of Discovery, began the expedition on May 14, 1804. They left from St. Louis, Missouri, and travelled up the Missouri River in three large boats. It was not easy to row the boats up the river. They had to use long poles to move the boats around rocks and fallen trees.

The Corps reached what is now North Dakota in October. They could not travel in winter, so they built Fort Mandan near the Mandan and Hidatsa Indian tribes. In November, they met French Canadian trader Toussaint Charbonneau and his Native American wife, Sacagawea. Charbonneau and Sacagawea joined the Corps as **interpreters**.

Fort Mandan is near today's Washburn, North Dakota. This photo shows a reconstruction of the fort.

To the Pacific!

The Corps left Fort Mandan in the spring of 1805. They reached the Rocky Mountains in August. Sacagawea helped them trade with the Shoshone for horses, which would help them in crossing the mountains. Even with the horses, crossing the Rockies was hard. They were nearly starving when they reached the other side in October. The Nez Percé Indians gave them food and shelter.

The Columbia River Gorge lies between the Columbia River and the Pacific Ocean. The Corps of Discovery traveled through here to reach the Pacific in November 1805.

Map of Lewis and Clark's Route

Fort Clatsop

Fort Mandan

Here you can see the route that the Corps of Discovery took during the expedition.

St. Louis

Key
— Lewis and Clark's route

The Corps made the last part of their journey on the Columbia River. They travelled in canoes. They reached the Pacific Ocean in November. In December 1805, they built Fort Clatsop in what is now Oregon. The Corps spent the winter at Fort Clatsop.

Returning Home

The Corps left Fort Clatsop in March 1806. They made it back to St. Louis in September. They had travelled over 8,000 miles (12,875 km). Lewis and Clark were welcomed back as heroes. They had brought back important information about the land, plants, and wildlife in the West.

Bighorn sheep were one of the animals that Lewis and Clark described in their journals.

These are flowers that Lewis and Clark collected and preserved during their journey.

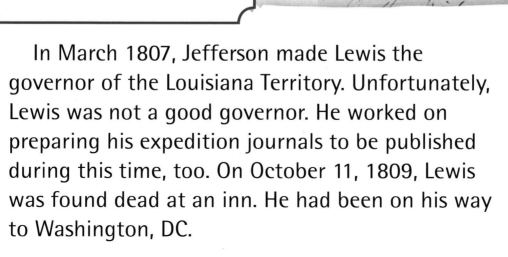

In March 1807, Jefferson made Lewis the governor of the Louisiana Territory. Unfortunately, Lewis was not a good governor. He worked on preparing his expedition journals to be published during this time, too. On October 11, 1809, Lewis was found dead at an inn. He had been on his way to Washington, DC.

Remembering Lewis and Clark

After the expedition, William Clark was a government agent in charge of dealing with Native Americans. Among his duties was making Native Americans give up their land and follow other orders from the US government. He tried to treat Native Americans with respect as he carried out these duties, though. He was also the governor of the Missouri Territory from 1813 until 1820. Clark died on September 1, 1838.

Today we remember these two great explorers in many ways. Many statues, parks, and museums can be found along the Lewis and Clark National Historic Trail, which stretches from Illinois to the Pacific Coast.

This statue of Lewis and Clark with Sacagawea stands at Fort Benton, in Montana.

Opening the West

The information that Lewis and Clark brought back from their expedition was an important first step in Westward Expansion. Because of Lewis and Clark, people knew that there was good land to farm and rivers that could be used for travel and shipping.

Pioneers began to settle west of the Mississippi. Often, this involved taking land that belonged to Native Americans. As more people came, territories became states. By 1900, the United States had states established from the Mississippi River to the Pacific Ocean.

These portraits of Lewis (left) and Clark (right) were painted around 1807, just after they returned from their expedition.

GLOSSARY

American Revolution (uh-MER-uh-ken reh-vuh-LOO-shun) Battles that soldiers from the colonies fought against Britain for freedom, from 1775 to 1783.

botany (BAH-tun-ee) The study of plants.

enlisted (in-LIST-ed) Joined the armed forces.

expedition (ek-spuh-DIH-shun) A trip for a special purpose.

frontier (frun-TEER) The edge of a settled country, where the wilderness begins.

interpreters (in-TER-prih-ters) People who help people who speak different languages talk to each other.

Louisiana Territory (loo-ee-zee-AN-uh TEHR-uh-tor-ee) Part of the land acquired by the United States in the Louisiana Purchase.

recruited (rih-KROOT-id) Convinced people to join your group.

stationed (STAY-shun-ed) Put someone in a certain place to do a job.

survive (sur-VYV) To live longer than, to stay alive.

Westward Expansion (WES-twurd ik-SPANT-shun) The continued growth of the United States by adding land to the west and having settlers move onto it.

INDEX

WEBSITES

Due to the changing nature of Internet links, PowerKids Press has developed an online list of websites related to the subject of this book. This site is updated regularly. Please use this link to access the list: www.powerkidslinks.com/pswe/lewcla/